M000084131

WISDOM FROM ABOVE

A STUDY IN JAMES

Lifetouch Series

Walking in the Spirit: A Study Through Galatians 5
Run the Race: A Study Through Hebrews 12
Wisdom from Above: A Study in James

WISDOM FROM ABOVE

A STUDY IN JAMES

STEVE PETTIT

journeyforth®
Greenville, South Carolina

The fact that materials produced by other publishers may be referred to in this volume does not constitute an endorsement of the content or theological position of materials produced by such publishers.

All Scripture is quoted from the King James Version unless otherwise noted. Scripture quotations marked ESV are from *The Holy Bible, English Standard Version*®, copyright © 2001 by Crossway Bibles, a publishing ministry of Good News Publishers. Used by permission. All rights reserved. Scripture quotations marked NASB are taken from the *New American Standard Bible*®, Copyright © 1960, 1962, 1963, 1968, 1971, 1972, 1973, 1975, 1977, 1995 by The Lockman Foundation. Used by permission.

Photo Credits: Steve Pettit ©2016, Hal Cook, BJU Marketing Communications

Wisdom from Above: A Study in James
Steve Pettit

Contributor: Eric Newton
Designer: Elly Kalagayan
Page layout: Michael Boone

Greenville, South Carolina 29614
JourneyForth Books is a division of BJU Press.

Printed in the United States of America

ISBN 978-1-62856-054-1
eISBN 978-1-62856-300-9

15 14 13 12 11 10 9 8 7 6 5 4 3

I dedicate this book to my first two pastors,
Dr. Wayne Thompson and Dr. Ed Nelson.
These men were living examples of strong conviction,
sincere compassion, and biblical wisdom.

CONTENTS

1
INTRODUCTION TO JAMES

God had been silent for four hundred years. His people wondered if His promises to Abraham and David were no longer valid. They chafed under the domination of Gentile overlords. The faithful among them, like Simeon and Anna (Luke 2:25, 36), longed to see the Messiah. And at exactly the right time, He came (Gal. 4:4). The divine silence had been deafening, but Jesus' arrival was the clearest, most personal message possible. After revealing Himself at many times and in many ways, our Creator finally spoke by His very own Son (Heb. 1:1–2).

This incarnation changed everything for those who had spiritual eyes to observe what was happening. Jesus Christ lived righteously, died vicariously, and arose victoriously. Redemption had dawned. Thousands and thousands of people believed in this Savior in the inaugural days of the church (Acts 2:41.)

But new life in Christ does not translate into an easy existence. There are trials and temptations, enemies and skeptics. How should Christians live in a world full of pressure? What does it mean to live by faith in contexts, both Jewish and Gentile, that are adverse to the gospel message? It requires wisdom from above. And that's exactly what we find at the heart of this letter.

New life in Christ does not translate into an easy existence.

The teaching of this letter seems to reverberate out from James 3:13–4:10. Before beginning our study of this passage, the letter's theological epicenter, it is important to become familiar with the context of the entire book, the surrounding region. We will begin to understand the letter's terrain as we orient ourselves to some of its key features. Let's start with James himself.

The Author: A Servant-Pastor

When James introduces himself as the author, he doesn't say which James he is, and there are at least three men named James in the New Testament:

- James the brother of John, the son of Zebedee
- James the son of Alphaeus, or James the Less
- James the half-brother of Jesus

It is clear from the book of Acts that by the time the epistle of James was written, James the brother of John had been martyred by Herod, the king of Israel. (See Acts 12:1–2.) James the Less is not likely to be the writer because little is known of his history. So tradition has established that the author is James, the half-brother of Jesus. Although he was not a believer in Jesus prior to Christ's crucifixion, James is mentioned in Matthew 13:55 and Mark 6:3. From Paul we learn that James trusted in his half-brother as Savior when Jesus appeared to him after the resurrection (1 Cor. 15:7).

Not only did James believe; he became an early leader of the church in Jerusalem. When Peter was miraculously released from prison by an angel, he instructed his fellow Christians, "Go shew these things unto James, and to the brethren" (Acts 12:17). Paul even refers to James as the only other one of the apostles, in addition to Peter, with whom he dialogued about the nature and sphere of gospel ministry (Gal. 1:19). The clearest indication of James' leadership is in Acts 15, when during the Jerusalem Council he gives wise counsel to help the church tread troubled waters and emerge in gospel unity. Therefore, there are good reasons to believe that Jesus' half-brother wrote the letter we know as James.

With his authorship in mind, think about how the letter begins: "James, a servant of God and of the Lord Jesus Christ" (James 1:1). He considers himself a bondslave not only of God the Father but also of his very own brother. James may have been a lead pastor in Jerusalem. He may have shared the same maternal gene pool as Jesus. He may have had a status nearly equivalent to Peter and John. However, he identifies himself as a slave. He glories in the reality that his life was not his own. And as will be explained below, his letter is not the collected wisdom of a revered leader but the application of truth spoken by his Messiah. James understood that he was a servant, not the master.

What is the value of knowing who wrote this book of the Bible?

—personal question —group question

The Audience: Brothers in Affliction

James is writing to Jewish believers of the dispersion—"the twelve tribes which are scattered abroad" (1:1). A great persecution had begun on the day of Stephen's stoning (Acts 8:1). Saul would later become the messenger of salvation to the Gentiles, but at this point in time he was the agent of persecution for believing Jews. They had been driven from their homes and were living outside of Israel (8:4). They scattered to places like Phoenicia, Cyprus, and Antioch (11:19).

Because of their forced dispersion, these believers were living wherever they could: in the forest, in refugee camps, or in the homes of other Jews. They were without jobs, living in poverty. The Jewish community rejected these believers because of their faith in Jesus as the Messiah. And they had little confidence that they would be able to return to their homes. It is to these people that James writes his letter, and his goal is clear.

James speaks to these people as a good shepherd does. Notice how he repeatedly refers to them as "(my beloved) brethren" (James 1:2, 16, 19; 2:1, 5, 14; 3:1; 4:11; 5:7, 12, 19). (*Brothers* is a general term that includes both male and female Christians.) Even though he may have been separated from his readers geographically, he identifies with them as fellow family members of God's church. He is not afraid to challenge these believers, but he does so lovingly. He writes as a fellow bondslave of Jesus Christ.

There is no better way to understand the context of a passage than by reading the book

in its entirety. Take twenty to twenty-five minutes and read James. Write down your observations about his audience and his reasons for writing to them.

The Message: Wholehearted Faithfulness

This letter was written approximately AD 40–45, making it the first New Testament book to be written. Some New Testament letters include extended explanations of key doctrines. Romans does this. Others concentrate on practical exhortations and read more like a sermon. James is in the latter category. In fact, some have considered James a manual for Christian Living 101. It contains over fifty imperatives, even though there are only 108 verses in the entire book. In other words, James assumes the content of the Christian faith and spends his time practically applying what it means to live out that faith as pilgrims in this world.

James introduces his message and purpose in the first eight verses of chapter one, where he addresses these dispersed believers on this issue: trials are a test of one's faith.

JAMES 1:1–8

> James, a servant of God and of the Lord Jesus Christ, to the twelve tribes which are scattered abroad, greeting. My brethren, count it all joy when ye fall into divers temptations; knowing this, that the trying of your faith worketh patience. But let patience have her perfect work, that ye may be perfect and entire, wanting nothing. If any of you

> lack wisdom, let him ask of God, that giveth to all men liberally, and upbraideth not; and it shall be given him. But let him ask in faith, nothing wavering. For he that wavereth is like a wave of the sea driven with the wind and tossed. For let not that man think that he shall receive any thing of the Lord. A double minded man is unstable in all his ways.

The primary purposes of these trials are to mature one's faith and develop one's character. This is very consistent with what Paul teaches concerning tribulation in Romans 5:3–5 and what Peter writes about suffering in 1 Peter 1:6–7.

The primary purposes of these trials are to mature one's faith and develop one's character.

Peter, James, and Paul are unified on this singular theme: believers must highly value these trials of life by counting them as joy. This is an act of faith and not feeling because trials are understood as the means of developing a believer's faith. God also promises His all-sufficient wisdom for every trial. He will guide us into making right choices all along the way if we seek and pursue this wisdom that is from above.

Read Romans 5:1–5. Write down the steps Paul mentions, starting with suffering and ending with hope. What truths in these verses provide assurance as we experience this process?

____

____

____

Describe in your own words God's purposes for your trials. Has there been a time when you have experienced this personally? If so, how did it help you grow?

In light of these truths, why would believers not value these trials and pursue God's wisdom? James 1:8 explains the reason. It is because of *double-mindedness*—a word coined by James. It means *two-souled* and has the idea of having a heart for God while at the same time having a heart for the world. John Bunyan called such a person "Mr. Facing-both-ways." The reason for the struggle is due to one's own inherent sinfulness. James uses three key words in his letter to describe these desires. In 1:14 *epithumia* means *lust; zelos* in 3:14 and 16 means *envy*; and *hedone* in 4:1 and 3 means *pleasures or lusts.* These desires can be satisfied only in this sinful world (Eph. 2:3; 1 John 2:16). So when do Christians waver in their faith? We waver when we fail to turn in self-denial from own self-centered desires. This is why worldliness is a very present and powerful problem in the church. It can be resolved only when we completely surrender ourselves to God and wholeheartedly and single-mindedly follow the Lord.

Look up Ephesians 2:3 and 1 John 2:16. What do these verses say about your sinful desires? What impact do lusts and pride have on your faith?

James begins his letter with encouragement to respond in faith when tested by trials. The letter reaches its climax in the section that we are studying, James 3:13–18. This passage is the **thematic peak** of the letter where James challenges God's people to be committed to being wise. This paragraph is followed by James 4:1–10, which serves as the **exhortational heart** of the book. As Douglas Moo explains, "James bursts out here with an expression of his deepest concern about the readers."[1] James expresses his concern in three ways:

1. He deals with the source of all conflicts among believers.
2. He addresses the problem of their worldliness.
3. He commands them to humbly turn to God in full surrender and complete repentance.

What links these challenges to the introductory section (James 1:1–8)?

[1] Douglas J. Moo, *The Letter of James*, The Pillar New Testament Commentary (Grand Rapids: Wm. Eerdmans Publishing Co., 2000), 45.

The Letter: Practical Exhortation

Douglas Moo presents three characteristics of James:[2]

1. It is "intensely practical." James uses clear and direct commands. His purpose is not so much to inform, but to chastise, exhort, and encourage. James concentrates on the outworking of theology.
2. It is concise and is similar to the book of Proverbs.
3. It is easy to understand and remember because of the "lavish use of metaphors and illustrations."

One interesting aspect of this letter is its frequent allusions to the Sermon on the Mount. For example, Jesus taught that disciples should rejoice amid trials (Matt. 5:12), and James echoes Him (James 1:2). Jesus calls for disciples to ask, because God the Father gives freely to them (Matt. 7:7). James speaks in the same terms (James 1:5; 4:2–3). With over twenty-five echoes of Jesus' most famous sermon, James' letter could be considered a commentary on the Sermon on the Mount. Jesus taught would-be disciples about the kingdom. They were interested in following Christ but did not yet understand what kind of king He was. James wrote to scattered disciples. They professed faith but were struggling with adversity and with worldliness.

[2] Ibid., 1–2.

We are very much like these believers James is addressing. We too are the church in the world. James' letter is ultimately a call to all believers throughout all church history to be totally loyal to the Lord, to pursue the goal of being spiritually mature, and to seek the wisdom that is from above.

What cultural pressures do Christians face today? Do we differ from what James' original readers experienced, and if so, how?

Recommended Reading

Before beginning the next chapter, read James 3:13–4:10. Note any themes or emphases that seem significant and list them below.

2
WHO IS A WISE MAN?

JAMES 3:13

Who is a wise man and endued with knowledge among you? let him shew out of a good conversation his works with meekness of wisdom.

Have you ever been on an airplane when a flight attendant comes over the intercom and urgently asks, "Is there a doctor on the plane?" What is everyone's immediate thought? Obviously, someone is in serious need of medical treatment. In chapter 3 and verse 13, James begins this section of his letter by asking a very urgent question: "Who is a wise man and endued with knowledge among you?" This revealing inquiry is intended to expose the serious need for wise leadership among God's people. James answers his own question by presenting the characteristics of a biblically wise person.

JAMES 3:13

Who is a wise man and endued with knowledge among you?

WORD STUDY

wise—possessing moral perception and discernment to handle practical matters

> **knowledge**—understanding gained by observation or study, like that needed by a teacher or resulting from special training; the insight or perception of an expert

James is probing with this question. He is addressing Jewish believers who were living as refugees outside of the land of Israel. They were from Jerusalem, and Acts 11:19 tells us they had been driven from their homes by intense religious persecution because of their faith in the Lord Jesus Christ. They were experiencing trials in multiple ways.

- Financially, they were poor.
- Emotionally, they were frustrated over their trying circumstances.
- Relationally, internal strife was brewing between believers.

The crying need was for wise leaders who could help God's people mature spiritually.

Are there people in your life who exercise wise leadership? How have they helped you mature spiritually? What do you think helped them develop moral discernment and insight?

What Is Wisdom?

Biblical wisdom is the practical application of Bible principles to real-life situations. Wise men and women have the experience and the expertise to lead and guide God's people to do the right thing. For example, James himself was an exemplary model of wisdom. As we noted earlier, he was the brother of Jesus (Gal. 1:19) and the leader of the church of Jerusalem. In AD 48–49, a turbulent theological storm arose in the early church concerning the Gentiles which threatened the unity and the future of the church. The question was this: Did a Gentile have to practice Jewish circumcision in order to be saved?

After much discussion and debate among the church leaders, including Peter and Paul, James stepped in and took the lead. "Men and brethren, hearken unto me" (Acts 15:13.) In his address, he reviewed the history of the powerful effects of the gospel among the Gentiles and concluded in Acts 15:19, "Therefore it is my judgment that we do not trouble those who are turning to God from among the Gentiles" (NASB).

James wisely concluded that a Gentile did not need to be circumcised in order to be a Christian. In addition, he recommended establishing four ethical guidelines for Gentile believers to observe in order not to offend their Jewish brethren—"abstain from pollutions of idols, and from fornication, and from things strangled, and from blood" (Acts 15:20). James's wise counsel was adopted and formulated in a letter to Gentile believers (15:23–29). Instead of being the seedbed of ongoing division, this first recorded church council came to a peaceful resolution and resulted in the advancement of the gospel throughout the world. The rest of the council concluded that James's proposal represented their interpretation of Scripture and agreed with the Holy Spirit (15:28). In other words, James had expressed "wisdom from above." He modeled wisdom by the way he led and guided God's people in applying biblical principles to real-life situations.

What have you learned from this glimpse into James's ministry? How could this glimpse help you navigate current situations you are facing?

What Are the Characteristics of a Wise Man?

JAMES 3:13

. . . let him shew out of a good conversation [beautiful lifestyle] . . .

WORD STUDY

let him shew—to demonstrate; to give proof; to make known; to give evidence (i.e., let his life and conduct be an example)

out of—from; by means of (i.e., from the good conduct the deeds of him)

good—beautiful; good

conversation—behavior; way of life

How can you tell a person is wise? James frames his initial answer to this question in the form of a command: "let him shew." Wisdom, first of all, displays itself in the way a person lives. James clearly establishes that wisdom is more than a matter of the intellect. Many have wrongly concluded that they cannot be wise because they do not have superior intellectual capability. James, being a Jew, operated from the mindset that wisdom has to do with one's moral and spiritual influence along with one's choices. Wisdom is a matter of the will, not just the mind.

In fact, what James says about wisdom is very close to what Paul says about the Spirit-filled life in Galatians 5:16–25. Both wisdom and Spirit-filled living involve the believer's yieldedness, obedience, and dependence on God.

Wisdom, first of all, displays itself in the way a person lives.

Read Galatians 5:16–25 and James 3:13–18. List the parallels between Spirit-filled living and wise living.

An even closer parallel to James' concept of wisdom is the emphasis of the book of Proverbs. Proverbs was written to give wisdom (Prov. 1:1–2). Wisdom is a gift from God (2:5–6) and is given to those who fear Him (1:7) and who earnestly pursue the knowledge of God (4:7). Similarly, James tells us that wisdom is given to those who wholeheartedly pursue God and who ask for wisdom in the midst of trials (James 1:2–8). For James, wisdom is demonstrated by moral and spiritual life that is attractively beautiful to both God and men.

Think of a situation when someone you know demonstrated wisdom. What was attractive about his behavior or words?

JAMES 3:13

. . . his works with meekness of wisdom.

WORD STUDY

works—deeds; accomplishments; actions

with— in connection with

meekness—gentleness; humility; courtesy; considerateness; mildness; modesty

Wisdom is demonstrated by handling life's issues with a meek spirit.

Secondly, you know wisdom not only by its actions but also by its attitude. Wisdom is demonstrated by handling life's issues with a meek spirit. Meekness has been described as the cardinal virtue of spiritual leadership. Numbers 12:3 says, "Now the man Moses was very meek, above all the men which were upon the face of the earth." Jesus said, "I am meek and lowly" (Matt. 11:29); and Paul spoke to the Corinthians by the "meekness and gentleness of Christ" (2 Cor. 10:1).

So what is meekness? It has often been falsely viewed as weakness because a meek person is gentle in his spirit. However, meekness actually involves great strength of character. A meek person must restrain his natural sinful desires and bring them into submission to God. A meek man is not rebellious or reactive; rather, he sweetly submits to God-given authority and yields to the demands and pressures of life that are placed upon him. He is not resentful toward those who mistreat him, and he does not become bitter toward God over the trying circumstances of life. Instead, he handles matters with a gentle, humble spirit. He is kind, thoughtful, and understanding of others' difficulties; he strives to do the biblically right thing in all situations; and ultimately, he works towards peaceful resolutions in all relationships.

Read through the preceding paragraph another time. Summarize in your own words the difference between **meekness** *and* **weakness.**

In the context of Numbers 12:3 Moses' siblings, Aaron and Miriam, are criticizing his leadership. What would be a meek response to the criticism of people close to you?

James begins James 3:13–4:10 with a command for all of God's people to seek to be wise. Wisdom is not a quality achieved by only a select few. Instead, it is to be the goal of all maturing, wholeheartedly committed believers.

What aspects of contemporary life and society make the development of wisdom so crucial?

In addition to those mentioned above, who else in Scripture displayed wisdom through virtuous choices and meek responses?

In what areas do you need wisdom in your life? What recent circumstances have exposed your need to grow in wisdom?

Recommended Reading

Before beginning the next chapter, read Colossians 3:5–9. Write out the characteristics of our old selves that we must put off.

3
WISDOM FROM BELOW

JAMES 3:14–16

But if ye have bitter envying and strife in your hearts, glory not, and lie not against the truth. This wisdom descendeth not from above, but is earthly, sensual, devilish. For where envying and strife is, there is confusion and every evil work.

We do what we do because we love what we love and think what we think. You can train a pet dog to react to various commands. But Fido's obedience or lack thereof is not the result of a reasoned worldview. We, on the other hand, are God's unique creation, His image-bearers. And God has given us the ability to reason—to live in light of the truth about Himself and His creation. We flourish when our lifestyle conforms to God's revealed point of view. Successful living flows from divine wisdom.

Successful living flows from divine wisdom.

All of our actions stem from our assumptions about life—governing principles known as *wisdom*. But a flourishing life is not guaranteed, because there is more than one kind of wisdom. In James 3:14–18, the author presents two kinds of life-governing wisdom. There is wisdom from above (that is, from God) that is on display when a person handles his issues with meekness (3:13, 17–18). In contrast, there is wisdom from below (that is, from fallen human nature and Satan). James begins by showing us the characteristics and consequences of one who is governed by this second kind of wisdom.

Wisdom from Below Stirs Up Trouble

JAMES 3:14

But if ye have bitter envying and strife in your hearts, glory not, and lie not against the truth.

WORD STUDY

bitter—harsh; resentful; the word indicates a harsh attitude

envying—jealousy; resentment; zeal, in a bad sense; fanatical zeal for an evil cause; a bitter aggressiveness

strife—selfish ambition; spirit of rivalry; resentfulness; hostility; faction; party spirit; selfishly seeking to gain an unethical advantage

glory—to brag; to be arrogant; to degrade; to look down; to make false claims for yourself; to assume superiority

lie—to be false; to deny the truth

against—in conflict with; in defiance of

truth—objective truth; revealed truth; the Christian faith

James is writing to a group of believers who were experiencing relational conflicts. It is not clear who was causing the problems. Perhaps the leaders were splitting the church into factions by their arrogant, abusive, agenda-driven words (3:1); or the church members may have been opposing the leadership and engaging in bitter partisan fights promoting their own views. In either case, the consequences of their actions reveal that there was a serious problem with the wisdom they were employing.

In verse 16, James says that their wisdom caused confusion and evil actions among believers. The Greek word for *confusion*, *akatastasia*, has the idea of disorder, instability, chaos, unsettledness, revolt, and tumult. (In 1 Corinthians 14:33, Paul reminds us, "God is not the author of confusion.") The consequences of their actions reveal that their wisdom was not from God. *Evil work* refers to actions or events that lack moral or spiritual value. They are simply worthless! This would include sins like suspicion, slander, gossip, hostile disputes, angry tempers, dissension, and an unhealthy craving for controversy (2 Cor. 12:20; 1 Tim. 6:4). In fact, by including the word *every*, James indicates that the kinds of bitter fruit grown from envy and strife are endless. When Satan sticks his nose into God's business, he always creates disturbances, disorder, and dissension among God's people. Turmoil in churches and families and relationships demonstrates a spirit opposed to God's plan.

Explain in your own words the relationship between Satan, earthly wisdom, and confusion.

James has already used the word translated* confusion *two times. Look up James 1:8 and 3:8. What do these references teach about these sources of instability?

James makes it clear that these problems do not come from people who have a meek spirit. Rather, "confusion and every evil work" come from those who are characterized by "bitter envying and strife." The ancient Greeks believed that envy was the moral cause of all human problems and conflicts. The second century moralist, Epictetus, said there was an organic relationship between envy and violence. He stated that Caesar could free people from "wars and fightings" but not from "envy."[1] Whenever there was a question concerning the origin of war, envy was the answer. But what does *envy* actually mean? Envy is an unhealthy craving that we attach to something we do not possess. It is a strong desire to gratify oneself and can include sensual pleasures, material possessions, or esteemed positions. Envy adds a harsh edge to covetousness that uses or abuses others for self-centered purposes.

Are there any relationships in which you have experienced disorder? Were jealousy and selfish ambition part of the problem? In what ways?

[1] *Discourses* 3.13.9, cited in Douglas Moo, *The Letter of James*, The Pillar New Testament Commentary (Grand Rapids: Eerdmans, 2000), 183.

Wisdom from Below Opposes God

JAMES 3:15–16

This wisdom descendeth not from above, but is earthly, sensual, devilish. For where envying and strife is, there is confusion and every evil work.

WORD STUDY

descendeth—comes down (the action is ongoing)

from above—from heaven (i.e., from God)

earthly—of the earth, earthbound; belonging to the world; produced by people opposed to God

sensual—in contrast with what is spiritual; from reasoning and feeling that are natural to fallen humanity

devilish—coming from unclean spirits, demons; the opposite of wisdom sent from God

for—because; for this reason

disorder—disturbance; confusion; chaos; disharmony; instability; unruliness; revolt; riot

evil—wicked; base; bad; foul; vile; worthless

work—matter; event; affair; action; practice

The "wisdom from below" is also characterized by selfish ambition (*strife*). In the days of Aristotle, *strife* often described a greedy, self-seeking politician pursuing political office by unfair means. Strife is a craving for self-glorification and is often seen in a jealous leader who forms a group and withdraws either emotionally or physically from the rest of the church. James says that if a believer harbors these attitudes in his heart, he cannot claim to be filled with the wisdom from God. This wisdom is **not** from above!

So what is the origin of this pseudo-wisdom, if it does not come from God? James lists three sources, which are progressively specific and damaging. First of all, this wisdom is *earthly*. In other words, it is "from below." It fails to account for God and spiritual realities. It is merely human thinking that is not influenced by divine revelation. It does not consider God's character or will in the matter of decision making and therefore handles issues and differences with a wrong spirit.

Secondly, this wisdom is *sensual*. Those operating according to this wisdom base their decisions on human reason or desires apart from the guidance of the Word of God and the Holy Spirit. Jude warned that sensuality characterized these leaders. "These be they who separate themselves, sensual, having not the Spirit" (Jude 1:19).

Finally, it is *devilish*, referring to demons or unclean spirits. This could mean that demons are inspiring this kind of wisdom or that this wisdom follows the way a demon thinks and acts. In either case, James detects the work of demons in disrupting the harmony and life of the church through the wrong kind of wisdom.

Worldly wisdom discounts God, goes for what feels good, and thinks like the Devil.

In summary, worldly wisdom discounts God, goes for what feels good, and thinks like the Devil. This "wisdom from below" is a way of thinking that flows directly from our three primary enemies: the world, the flesh, and the Devil. No wonder James is concerned that this mindset not characterize our everyday choices.

Think of a recent story that has grabbed headlines. What kind of wisdom was on display? How do you know? How can you learn from this?

James contrasts this negative type of wisdom with the wisdom that is from above, which is demonstrated by a spirit of meekness. In chapter 4 James commands God's people to forsake this envy and selfish ambition by resisting the Devil and submitting themselves to God. It is instructive that God commands Christians to *submit* ourselves to Him and *resist* Satan. The Lord knows that our flesh is bent the opposite way—to resist God and submit ourselves to Satan. The Devil's wisdom is doubly appealing to us when we consciously choose not to submit to God and His wisdom. When we ignore God and go with our own reasoning and instincts, we are opening ourselves up to demonic thinking.

If God's wisdom is clearly superior to earthly wisdom, why don't we submit to it? In what ways has this been a struggle for you?

Can Satan influence a believer? To what degree can a believer's thinking be used by the Evil One to accomplish his purposes?

Write down at least two biblical examples of when God's people refused to submit to God and came under the influence of worldly, fleshly, demonic thinking. What can be learned from these examples?

Recommended Reading

Before beginning the next chapter, read Matthew 5:3–12 and Galatians 5:22–23. What are the characteristics that should be true of Christ's disciples?

4
WISDOM FROM ABOVE

JAMES 3:17–18

But the wisdom that is from above is first pure, then peaceable, gentle, and easy to be intreated, full of mercy and good fruits, without partiality, and without hypocrisy. And the fruit of righteousness is sown in peace of them that make peace.

There is a centuries-old saying, "The proof of the pudding is in the eating." In other words, a cook can insist she has made something good. But the test of her success is when someone actually tastes the food. (Have you ever put food on your plate, only to find that it tasted far worse than it looked?) We can insist we are wise, but how we actually live—especially how we relate to others—is the true test. A wise man is identified by the quality of life he lives and the manner in which he handles life's issues. In the verses following his description of wisdom from below, James unfolds in careful detail the specific qualities that reflect this heavenly wisdom.

The Divine Source of Wisdom

JAMES 3:17

But the wisdom that is from above . . .

WORD STUDY

wisdom—the moral skill based on divine principles that is necessary to live successfully

First of all, the "wisdom from above" originates with God (3:17). James has already stated that wisdom is found in God: "Every good gift and every perfect gift is from above, and cometh down from the Father of lights, with whom is no variableness, neither shadow of turning" (1:17). God has also revealed that He delights to give His children wisdom in answer to their prayers: "If any of you lack wisdom, let him ask of God, that giveth to all men liberally, and upbraideth not; and it shall be given him" (1:5). True wisdom does not come through intellectual effort but through humble and prayerful dependence.

The connection between wisdom and prayer surfaces frequently in Scripture. For example, when faced with the daunting task of governing Israel, Solomon asked the Lord for wisdom instead of riches, honor, and fame. This prayer honored God and was favorably answered (1 Kings 3:3–14). Paul prayed this way for the Colossians, whom he apparently did not even know personally. He explains that his struggle in prayer is for them to have spiritual wisdom, which is found ultimately in Christ (Col. 2:1–3). James himself exemplified this kind of prayer life. Church history remembers him by the nickname "Camel Knees" because of the time he invested in praying on his knees in the temple. Wisdom is God's gift to His people as an answer to their prayers.

Read Colossians 1:9–14 and 2:1–3. What do these references say about divine wisdom?

Since heavenly wisdom is dependent on a prayer-filled life, what changes do you need to make to apply the wisdom from above?

The Essential Quality of Wisdom

JAMES 3:17

But the wisdom that is from above is first pure . . .

Secondly, James lists a catalogue of virtues that result from wisdom. He heads the list with wisdom's primary quality—*purity*. By singling out purity, James clearly distinguishes God's wisdom with wisdom from below, which comes from impure sources—the world, the flesh, and the Devil—and bears impure fruit: bitterness and animosity. In contrast, wisdom from above is pure in both a moral and a devotional sense.

Morally, this purity means freedom from all defilement, including jealousy, selfish ambition, and sexual immorality. We as believers can experience this pureness only through the blood of Jesus Christ cleansing us from our sins (Heb. 9:14). As a result, God has imparted His own nature to us (2 Peter 1:4), and we now have a new spiritual nature with a new ability to live a morally virtuous life (James 1:18, 21; Eph. 4:22–24).

Devotionally, this purity entails a single-minded, passionate pursuit to know God and obey His Word. We experience continual cleansing through studying and meditating on the Scriptures (John 15:3; 17:17). As we grow in our knowledge of the Word, we develop an ever-increasing sensitivity to the polluting influences of the world's thoughts, words, and actions (James 1:27). The more we drink from the living streams of God's holy Word (Ps. 1:3), the more renewed we will be by its purity (19:8).

Read Matthew 5:8 and Hebrews 12:14. What emphasis does God place on purity? How can purity be made a priority? What about the preceding paragraph is most convicting?

Look up John 15:3, John 17:17, James 1:27, Psalms 1:3, and Psalms 19:8. Write out one of the verses below. Meditate on this passage this week.

The Virtuous Evidences of Wisdom

JAMES 3:17

But the wisdom that is from above is first pure, then peaceable, gentle, and easy to be intreated, full of mercy and good fruits, without partiality, and without hypocrisy.

The more we drink from the living streams of God's holy Word, the more renewed we will be by its purity.

Thirdly, this heavenly wisdom is characterized by six qualities that concern our interpersonal relationships with others. These virtues further describe various aspects of the moral and devotional purity mentioned first. James uses an alliterated style by using *e* in the first four virtues and *a* in the last two. Notice the emphasis on peace at the beginning of this catalog in verse 17, as well as at the end of verse 18. James seems to be emphasizing the primary issue by which this congregation was demonstrating worldly wisdom. They lacked peace.

Six Virtues

1. **Peaceable** (*eirēnikē*)—People of wisdom are peacemakers instead of strife-causers. They seek to settle disputes instead of provoking them.
2. **Gentle** (*epieikēs*)—Wise people respect the feelings of others, make allowances for their weaknesses, and avoid being severe and stern when dealing with others.
3. **Easy to be entreated** (*eupeithēs*)—A wise person is open to reason and willing to listen and cooperate

when a better way is shown, as long as Scriptural principles are not being violated.

4. **Full of mercy and good fruits** (*eleous*)—A wise person's life is one of compassion in action. He seeks to help those who are needy or in distress with acts of mercy.
5. **Without partiality** (*adiakritos*)—A wise person is straightforward and consistent in his positions without wavering. He treats people the same and resists showing favoritism to one group of people over another.
6. **Without hypocrisy** (*anupokritos*)—A wise person is free from pretense and has no hidden agendas. He does not manipulate people to accomplish his self-centered purposes. He is willing to trust God to change people.

Does your life evidence this kind of virtuous fruit? Is there a lack of virtue in one or more of these areas that indicates you may be relying on worldly wisdom? In what areas is God growing you?

Read James 3:17–18, Matthew 5:3–12, and Galatians 5:22–23. What similarities do you find in these three passages—James's list of virtues, the Beatitudes, and the fruit of the Spirit?

The Powerful Effects of Wisdom

JAMES 3:18

And the fruit of righteousness is sown in peace of them that make peace.

WORD STUDY

fruit—harvest; result; outcome; product; this word refers to the seed which results in the fruit

righteousness—doing what is right, what God requires; goodness; justice

sown—distributed (as seed; refers to a customary practice)

peace—tranquility; peace in the community

make—to bring about; to practice; to cultivate (indicates characteristic behavior)

Wisdom from above comes to fruition in peace and righteousness.

Finally, James reveals the powerful effects of this kind of wisdom. Using a farming metaphor, he describes the result of a wise man's actions before he ever makes a single choice—sowing and cultivating. James is confident that there will be a guaranteed harvest of righteous living among God's people if the congregation is guided and governed by peace. If we characteristically plant seeds of wise, gentle, sincere peace, the fruit that crops up will be practical righteousness in the likeness of Jesus Christ (Rom. 6:18; Eph.

4:24). Whereas wisdom from below results in "confusion and every evil work" (James 3:16), wisdom from above comes to fruition in peace and righteousness. The proof of the wisdom that guides us is in our response to life's pressures, particularly in relation to believers around us.

In 1 Thessalonians 5:13 Paul says to "be at peace among yourselves." Is there anyone right now with whom you are at odds? If so, read Matthew 5:23–24. What should you do?

Why do you think righteousness grows in contexts where believers are striving for peace with one another?

Recommended Reading

Before beginning the next chapter, read Galatians 5:13–26 and write down what Paul says about the flesh, which is in combat with the Spirit.

5
THE SOURCE OF CONFLICT

JAMES 4:1–3

From whence come wars and fightings among you? come they not hence, even of your lusts that war in your members? Ye lust, and have not: ye kill, and desire to have, and cannot obtain: ye fight and war, yet ye have not, because ye ask not. Ye ask, and receive not, because ye ask amiss, that ye may consume it upon your lusts.

Historians estimate that 200 million people died in war or oppression in the twentieth century alone.[1] Thousands of U.S. military personnel have died in the War on Terror, launched by President George Bush after the terrorist attacks of September 11, 2001. Nearly 1.1 million violent crimes were committed in the United States in 2013.[2] Tragically, wars and fighting have been part of human history ever since Cain murdered Abel as recorded in Genesis 4.

James has already portrayed the devastating results of human wisdom among God's people (3:14–16). Now he explains that the dissension in this early church stemmed from the same evil that is the source of all human conflict. Where do wars and fights come from? This question has plagued humanity

[1] http://necrometrics.com/all20c.htm

[2] http://www.fbi.gov/about-us/cjis/ucr/crime-in-the-u.s/2013/crime-in-the-u.s.-2013/tables/table-12/table_12_crime_trends_by_population_group_2012-2013.xls

down through the ages. Before the time of Christ, Herodotus—the "Father of History" (484–425 BC)—wrote a book called *Histories.* In this work, he conducted a historical investigation into the cause of war, concluding that wars were caused by the relentless drive for power or imperialism. Thucydides (460–395 BC) followed Herodotus as a historian. When speaking of war and human suffering, Thucydides said they "always will occur as long as the nature of mankind remains the same . . . the cause of all these evils [is] the lust for power arising from greed and ambition."[3] Not surprisingly, James gives similar answers alongside these famous historians as to the cause of conflict; the difference is that his answer is divinely inspired. James observes the symptom of conflict and diagnoses what causes it.

How are interpersonal conflicts similar to military battles? How are they different?

The Root Issue

JAMES 4:1

From whence come wars and fightings among you?

[3] Robert B. Strassler, *The Landmark Thucydides* (New York: Simon and Schuster, 1996), 427.

WORD STUDY

from whence—from where; what is the source or cause?

wars—conflicts; quarrels; struggles; continuing enmity; a series of disputes

fightings—battles; quarrels; disputes; the reference is to a specific, intense outburst

First of all, James observes that human conflicts are rooted in the sinful desires that arise within our evil, corrupt hearts. James' rhetorical question literally reads, "From where wars? From where fightings?" His direct answer is also in the form of a question: "Come they not hence: from your lusts that war in your members?" (4:1). The *hence* is pointing the finger at the source of the conflicts. It is found in the inner cravings of the human heart. These are pleasure-oriented desires for personal satisfaction and sensual indulgence.

> **The source of tension comes from these self-centered lusts that have not been subdued and reengineered by the grace of God.**

God created the human body with innate desires. It is natural for a thirteen-year-old boy to be hungry, often! It is natural for a young adult man and woman to desire an intimate physical relationship with one another. It is natural for an outdoorsman to want to climb the Rocky Mountain summit. God made us with desires strong enough to pursue life-sustaining nourishment and procreative relationships and awe-inspiring physical challenges. The problem is not that we desire things that bring pleasure. The problem is that we pursue pleasure for the wrong purposes or in the wrong ways. We go far beyond nourishment to gluttony. We choose immoral intimacy over God's beautiful design for marriage. We make physical accomplishments about ourselves instead of God. And these misplaced desires are so pervasive that the New Testament never uses this term *pleasures* (*ēdonōn*)—from which we derive our term *hedonism*—in a positive light.

Read Titus 3:3. How does it describe what we were before we were rescued by God our Savior, who is good and merciful? Notice especially the devastating interpersonal results of our hedonism.

What innate desires are you tempted to pursue for wrong purposes or in wrong ways? What conflict has this caused for you personally or interpersonally?

How then do things go so wrong if what God made is so good? James uses the metaphor of a war to describe the way in which these desires operate. Lusts are like soldiers who use the various parts of the human body as their weapons. These desires fight for their own gratification, and they create multiple problems for believers. There is an inner spiritual conflict between the desires of the flesh and the desires of the Spirit of God (Gal. 5:17). The believer's conscience sounds off like an alarm system against these evil desires. Inevitably, outer conflicts will arise among believers because of these carnal appetites. James has already stated that controversies, quarrels, animosities, and bad feelings come from envy and selfish ambition. The source of tension comes from these self-centered lusts that have not been subdued and reengineered by the grace of God.

Read Galatians 5:19–21. What do you notice about the works of the flesh listed? What God-given desires are misplaced or perverted, resulting in these works?

The Progression

JAMES 4:1

. . . come they not hence, even of your lusts that war in your members?

WORD STUDY

hence—from this; from this source

lusts—desires for pleasure; cravings; appetites; passions

war—to make war; to wage war; to be at war; to battle; to be in conflict; to campaign (refers to a continuing action)

members—parts of your body; your own selves

Secondly, James reveals the process that leads from inner frustration to outward conflict (4:2). The word *hence* carries forward the thought of the preceding question *from whence* and points the way to the answer by emphasizing the source. This process begins with inner sinful desires. James uses two words to describe them: "You *lust*" and "You are *envious*." Lust simply means strong desires. Envy is the passionate desire within a person to obtain (literally "to attach itself to") what he doesn't possess. These are ongoing, present lusts that are not being fulfilled and that are producing a sense of inner frustration. Four different times James expresses the disappointment of thwarted desires: "have not," "desire to have, and cannot obtain," "have not," and "receive not" (4:2–3). The result of these frustrated desires is a pursuit of satisfaction at all costs, leading in the end to relational conflicts: fighting, killing, and war. These words could be literal, but more likely James is using them metaphorically to describe the emotional and verbal quarrels that splinter the people of God. James takes our seemingly minor squabbles to another level by showing us how horrible these things look in the eyes of God. This also falls in line with what Jesus says in Matthew 5:21–22 when He quotes the sixth commandment, "Thou shalt not kill," as a cause for judgment. James then interprets the heart of the law by declaring that even anger and derogatory name-calling are worthy of God's judgment. But ultimately, he is depicting the process of human conflicts with this purpose in mind: to reveal that change in our relationships can come only through a change of our hearts.

What do personal lusts (i.e., misplaced desires) have to do with interpersonal conflict? Discuss tangible examples that illustrate the relationship.

Failed Opportunities

JAMES 4:2–3

Ye lust, and have not: ye kill, and desire to have, and cannot obtain: ye fight and war, yet ye have not, because ye ask not. Ye ask, and receive not, because ye ask amiss, that ye may consume it upon your lusts.

WORD STUDY

lust—to desire greatly; to continually want or long for

have—to possess; to acquire; to have satisfaction

kill—to commit murder; to resort to murder

desire—to be filled with jealousy; to be envious; to be zealous or have an ambition to fulfill desires

obtain—acquire; satisfy one's desire

fight—to battle by force; to quarrel, dispute, engage in disputes; to clash severely

war—to engage in conflicts; to strive

ask not—fail to ask for oneself; do not pray

amiss—with wrong motives; in the wrong spirit; incorrectly

that—for the purpose of

consume—spend completely; waste; squander; indulge

lusts—desires; passions

Finally, James declares that these conflicts are due to spiritual shortcomings. Remember the preceding points. Our desires are strong and, by nature, misaligned with God's purposes. We want to fulfill our flesh as we see fit. And when this drive for pleasure becomes thwarted, frustration builds up and explodes into conflict with others. It's a seemingly hopeless situation. If such problems cropped up in the early church, before the advent of online photos and videos, YouTube, and Instagram, what hope do we have of combatting these temptations? There *is* hope, of course (for example, 1 Cor. 10:13), but we cannot overlook the spiritual advantages that these believers failed to utilize.

All prayer requires a submission of one's desires to the will of God.

James mentions two defects. First of all, we are ripe for conflict when we fail to come to God with sanctified desires: "Ye have not, because ye ask not" (4:2). All prayer requires a submission of one's desires to the will of God (1 John 5:14–15). Therefore, if you do not pray, you are either trusting in your own self-sufficiency, or you simply do not want to yield your desires to God. He has told us to come boldly to His throne of grace for mercy and help in time of need (Heb. 4:16). The power to overcome fleshly desires is available in Jesus Christ. If we are fighting instead of peacemaking, one reason may be that we are not submitting ourselves to God and asking for wisdom.

What areas of spiritual growth have been struggles for you recently? How frequently and specifically have you been praying about them? Write out what you should do.

There is a second defect. Sometimes we ask, but we do not receive because of wrong motives: "Ye ask, and receive not, because ye ask amiss, that ye may consume it upon your lusts" (4:3). We may seem to pray sincerely, but we actually intend to *spend* the answer to our prayers on gratifying self-centered appetites. God doesn't give things that are contrary to His revealed will. Nor does He give us things that are not in line with His directive will for our lives. Prayer includes both submitting our desires to God and trusting that He knows what is best for us. It means soberly evaluating why we want what we want. F. J. A. Hort wrote,

> God bestows not gifts only, but the enjoyment of them: but ***the enjoyment which contributes to nothing beyond itself is not what He gives in answer to prayer***; and petitions to him which have no better end in view are not prayers.[4]

Human conflicts, including those inside the church, can be resolved if believers will fully yield themselves to God with a single-minded, wholehearted purpose to love Him supremely and honor Him with their lives. Otherwise, the genetic defect of sinful desires and the lack of exercise in humble prayer will consistently result in conflict.

[4] Fenton Hort, ed., *The Epistle of St. James* (London: Macmillan & Co., 1909), 91. Emphasis added.

Think of examples of prayers that amount to intentions to gratify selfish desires. How could those illegitimate prayers be turned into genuine petitions?

According to James 4, what is the source of every human conflict? Put the answer in your own words.

Do you have desires that you refuse to bring to God? If so, why do you think this is the case?

Recommended Reading

Before beginning the next chapter, scan the biblical testimony about Lot in Genesis 13:5–13; 14:12–17; 18:16–33; and especially 19:1–38. List some possible connections between Lot's life and worldliness today.

6
WORLDLINESS

JAMES 4:4

Ye adulterers and adulteresses, know ye not that the friendship of the world is enmity with God? whosoever therefore will be a friend of the world is the enemy of God.

Now we come to the heart and core of the book of James. The author puts his finger on the central struggle that God's people have with their Savior: worldliness. James has alluded to this problem at points throughout the epistle. For example, he declares that believers are double-minded (1:8) when they ask God for wisdom during trials, yet at the same time doubt Him when they pray. He is not speaking of the common doubts that all believers experience when they pray (Mark 9:24). Rather, James is saying that a double-minded man is a person who is conflicted in his soul over his allegiance to God. He is torn between sin and obedience. Instead of being totally committed to God, he vacillates in his heart because of his craving for the things of this world (James 1:14–15; 1 John 2:15–17). The double-minded person is reluctant to let go of the pleasures of this world for the demands of discipleship. James depicts this same conflict later on in the book (James 3:13–4:3). He describes this struggle with selfish desires in various ways: the earthly wisdom that has created instability among believers (3:14–16), the wars and fights that are ongoing because of the lusts in our hearts (4:1–2), and the unanswered prayers that are full of self-centered desires (4:3). James repeatedly uses three words to describe the self-centered desires that are in all believers: *lust*, *envy*, and *pleasures*. The letter reaches a milestone in James 4:4 when the author confronts the shocking reality of worldliness within the lives of believers.

What Is Worldliness?

JAMES 4:4
Ye adulterers and adulteresses, know ye not that the friendship of the world is enmity with God?

WORD STUDY

adulteresses—unfaithful wives

know—to understand; to comprehend; to realize; to be aware

friendship—affection; love; close relationship

world—world system; the affairs of mankind apart from God and hostile to God; the corrupt part of culture controlled by Satan

enmity—hostility, hatred; the opposite of friendship

The double-minded person is reluctant to let go of the pleasures of this world for the demands of discipleship.

What is the *world*? In this passage, the *world* does not refer to the planet God created or to all the nations around the globe. The term world means the unregenerate people (Eph. 2:1–2) who live under the control of Satan (1 John 5:19) and who have structured life to make self-indulgence and self-aggrandizement their central aims (2:15–17). This includes the values, motives, morals, pursuits, and prejudices that mold and control the affairs of unsaved people. In his book *Love Not the World: Winning the War Against Worldliness*, Randy Leedy describes the world as "the lost people of our generation, especially as they manifest their estrangement from our Father by developing and pursuing values that are contrary to the biblical morality that reflects His character."[1]

Based on the descriptions of the world in the preceding paragraph, write down some aspects of the world you see in contemporary life.

The mindset of the world towards God and His will is one of either apathetic disregard or of open hostility, thus making the world the enemy of God. The lives of those who follow God will stand in contrast to the lifestyle of the world. Was worldliness a genuine problem for New Testament believers? Twice in this verse James accuses professing Christians of having an affectionate relationship with the world: "the friendship of the world" and "a friend of the world." Apparently, the influence of the world was significant enough to prompt James to write about it.

[1] Randy Leedy, *Love Not the World: Winning the War Against Worldliness* (Greenville: BJU Press, 2012), 13.

If the *world* is unsaved humanity in its opposition to God's authority and moral character, what is *worldliness*? James describes it in two relational terms: *adultery* and *friendship*. When James calls believers *adulteresses*, he is employing Old Testament language. God called Israel His bride (Isa. 54:5), and their marriage covenant demanded unswerving loyalty to Jehovah. When Israel turned to worship of idols, they were, in effect, committing spiritual adultery. James labels these Jewish believers *adulteresses* because they were pursuing the carnal attractions of this sinful world like Israel pursued idols. In other words, we as believers exhibit worldliness by the direction of our affections.

Hosea 2:16 reads: "And it shall be at that day, saith the Lord, that thou shalt call me Ishi [my husband]; and shalt call me no more Baali [my Baal]." What does this verse say about God's commitment to Israel? What significance does this have for your relationship with God?

James also calls these believers the "friend[s] of the world." In Middle Eastern culture, friendship is taken very seriously. Friends identify with one another. They share the same values and loyalties. To choose to be someone's friend is a binding commitment. In other words, this passage teaches that worldliness includes choosing to share the standards, priorities, and pursuits of this fallen world system. If we embrace the lifestyle characteristics of the world, will we not soon lose our identity as children of God?

The recommended reading at the end of Chapter 5 was the account of Lot in Genesis. What does the biblical testimony about Lot have to do with James' statement about being "a friend of the world"?

How Does Worldliness Evolve?

JAMES 4:4

. . . whosoever therefore will be a friend of the world is the enemy of God.

WORD STUDY

therefore —consequently

will—to intend; to purpose; to desire; to deliberate to the point of choosing

is—to cause oneself; to establish oneself; to designate oneself; to commit oneself; to take one's stand as (indicates a continuing status)

enemy—one who is hostile

How do believers become worldly? James asks another rhetorical question (note also 3:13; 4:1): "Know ye not that the friendship of the world is enmity with God?" His answer reveals that worldliness is a matter of choice. "Whosoever therefore will be a friend of the world is the enemy of God."

The path to worldliness involves four stages. First, worldliness *begins* with our inherent sinful desires.

> But every man is tempted, when he is drawn away of his own lust, and enticed. (James 1:14)

We constantly engage in warfare on two fronts. Internally, we are seized by the self-centered inclinations of our own flesh. Is your heart set on becoming spiritually mature or on satisfying your own lusts? What do you truly value? What is your priority? Are you double-minded (in other words, two-souled—having a heart for God and a heart for the world)? Or are you single-mindedly committed to following Christ? Worldliness starts in the realm of our desires.

What values and motivations and attitudes typify the world today? Where do you find them showing up in your own desires or in the pursuits of those around you?

Second, worldliness *develops* through a period of deliberation. A timeframe often exists during which we struggle with our desires before making an actual choice. Our hearts become a battle zone between the commands of God and our sinful desires. The choice is ours (1:14). At this point, if we deliberate too long with our self-indulgent desires, they eventually wear down our resistance to the temptation.

Third, worldliness *solidifies* into a conscious decision to be a friend of the world. The word for *will* means making a choice at a definite point in time. When we reach this verdict, our allegiance has shifted, and we have established ourselves as friends of the world.

Is your heart set on becoming spiritually mature or on satisfying your own lusts?

Finally, worldliness *manifests* itself in actions and behavior. To enter into a friendship with the world means that we are allowing the world's way of thinking to mold and shape our motives, pursuits, activities, and even our appearance.

> And be not conformed to this world: but be ye transformed by the renewing of your mind, that ye may prove what is that good, and acceptable, and perfect, will of God. (Rom. 12:2)

How do various contemporary activities or styles of living relate to worldliness?

What is the result of worldliness? The believer establishes himself as the enemy of God. And as strange as this may sound, every believer needs to be warned of this reality: "Know ye not that the friendship of the world is enmity with God?" (4:4). The verb *know* is in the perfect tense, meaning that this truth is learned and should continue to be a controlling reality throughout the Christian journey. We must always realize that we cannot be friends of the world and remain the friends of

God. Those who do become friends of the world have taken on the identity of God's enemies. Man initiates this enmity, but God then distances Himself from the believer, and no close, intimate relationship can then exist with God.

Consider John's description in 1 John 2:16 of "all that is in the world, the lust of the flesh, and the lust of the eyes, and the pride of life." How does choosing these elements of the world affect our relationship with God?

Discuss the period of deliberation when a believer is wrestling with trusting God or yielding to evil desires.

Has this explanation of James 4:4 exposed worldliness in your heart or lifestyle? In what ways? If so, confess your sin and be renewed in your relationship with God.

Recommended Reading

Before beginning the next chapter, read Ephesians 5:22–33. In this passage Paul gives inerrant directions for husbands and wives. These commands are important, not only for interpersonal harmony but also because the marriage relationship pictures Christ and His Church. List ways in which the instructions for husbands and wives teach us about Christ's love for us and our love for Him.

7
GOD'S RESPONSE TO WORLDLINESS

JAMES 4:5–6

Do ye think that the scripture saith in vain, The spirit that dwelleth in us lusteth to envy? But he giveth more grace. Wherefore he saith, God resisteth the proud, but giveth grace unto the humble.

There is hardly a more important theme in Scripture than the loyal love of God. For example, the Lord promises David that his dynasty will rule an everlasting kingdom (2 Sam. 7). The promise will not be fulfilled because David's descendants were faithful, but because God's love is loyal. One of the most powerful illustrations of loyal love in the New Testament is found in Luke 15. In this story Jesus portrays repentant sinners coming home to God like a prodigal son coming home to his father. God loves and welcomes us home with open arms and rejoicing, in spite of our foolish infidelity. This poignant story is repeated every time a sinner repents and is made alive (Luke 15:10, 32). Like He did with Israel, God chooses to set His love upon us, his wayward children (Deut. 7:7–8). He stakes His character on the fulfillment of His promises to His people. It is a trustworthy saying: "If we believe not, yet he abideth faithful: he cannot deny himself" (2 Tim. 2:13). It is this theme of loyal love to which James turns to explain God's response to worldliness.

God is both jealous and gracious.

After exposing the lamentable nature of worldliness among believers, James pronounces a sharp denunciation of their spiritual adultery, intending to show them the true nature of their choice to be the world's friends (James 4:4). Now the author establishes, with a biblical precedent and promise, God's desire and ability to bring believers back into spiritual oneness with Him. Christians can recover from worldliness because God is both jealous and gracious.

God Is Jealous

JAMES 4:5

Do ye think that the scripture saith in vain, The spirit that dwelleth in us lusteth to envy?

WORD STUDY

think—to suppose; imagine; consider; believe

in vain—in an empty manner; for no purpose; to no effect; for nothing

dwelleth—to make; to dwell; to implant

lusteth—to long for; to desire; to be filled with desire; to claim

to—to the point of

envy—legitimate, passionate jealousy

God is jealous, with a passionate zeal for His own character and glory. God reveals Himself to His people through His law (Torah), and God's people manifest their love for God by passionately seeking to know and obey the law of God (Deut. 6:4–9). When God's people turned away from the law and began to seek after idols, God was not apathetic towards their apostasy.

He fervently and zealously pursued them, longing for their hearts to return to Him with a broken spirit and a full submission to His Word. This is the primary point of James 4:5—God is jealous for believers' hearts.

James expects his readers to understand this righteous, divine jealousy because it is scriptural. However, it takes a little work to follow James's argument. Verse 5 is considered one of the more difficult verses in the New Testament to interpret for two reasons. First, James says, "Do ye think that the scripture [the Old Testament] saith in vain," yet there is no verse that can be found in the Old Testament that makes this exact statement. Secondly, the precise meaning of the phrase, "The spirit that dwelleth in us lusteth to envy," can be interpreted in a number of ways, making it challenging to discern its exact meaning. Both points require further explanation.

First of all, the Scripture to which James refers is not a direct quote of a particular verse; it is instead a general truth about God's relationship with His people that surfaces throughout Scripture. There is precedent for James's words to New Testament believers, because the Old Testament clearly establishes a pattern of how God responds when His people are unfaithful.

> Thou shalt not bow down thyself to them, nor serve them: for I the Lord thy God am a jealous God, visiting the iniquity of the fathers upon the children unto the third and fourth generation of them that hate me. (Ex. 20:5)
>
> For thou shalt worship no other god: for the Lord, whose name is Jealous, is a jealous God. (Ex. 34:14)
>
> Thus saith the Lord of hosts; I was jealous for Zion with great jealousy, and I was jealous for her with great fury. (Zech. 8:2)

God also graphically illustrated this pattern by commanding the Old Testament prophet Hosea to marry a prostitute named Gomer. Through this prophet's marriage God pictured the tragedy of Israel's unfaithfulness to Him when they pursued Baal and other false gods. This example, along with the Old Testament statements, demonstrates God's unchanging, jealous nature. The Lord is jealous for the affections of believers just as a husband is righteously jealous for the faithful affections of his wife.

Can jealousy be a good thing? If so, under what circumstances? What would it mean if God were not jealous for the affections of His people?

James describes God's jealousy when he says, "The spirit that dwelleth in us lusteth to envy" (4:5). The key to understanding this phrase is determining the subject of the sentence. There are two primary options:

Option 1: The subject is the spirit of man that God caused to dwell in us. This spirit of man envies intensely, which causes conflicts like those mentioned earlier in this passage.

Option 2: The subject is God, who jealously longs for the spirit He made (that dwells in us) to be wholly committed to the Father.

If the first option captures James's meaning, then this statement means that the human spirit lusts with envy. While our spirits can lust with envy, this interpretation doesn't make the best sense in light of James' direction. He is describing God's desire toward His erring people. In context, James has been addressing the problem of the believer's worldliness. God's desire is for man to be wholeheartedly committed to Him. It is also clear that God is the one who makes the spirit to dwell in us, whether it is the human spirit or the Holy Spirit. In addition, in the next verse (4:6), God is clearly the subject. Therefore, it makes more contextual sense that God is the subject of this phrase.

The primary verb in this sentence is *lusteth* or *yearns*. The verb *envy* refers to divine jealousy. The ESV reads, "He yearns jealously over the spirit that he has made to dwell in us" (4:5). The *spirit* could be the Holy Spirit implanted in the soul at regeneration or the human spirit given to man at creation. Since God is going to give believers a series of commands calling for a heart of humility before God (4:7–10), it seems best to view *spirit* as referring to the human spirit. So, ultimately, James is telling us that God jealously desires the undivided love and loyalty of His people.

In a fast-paced, busy world, how can you give undivided love to the Lord?

Think about the reality of God's loyal love for His people and the necessity of our loyal love for Him. How do they relate? What significance does this have for you today?

God Is Gracious

JAMES 4:6

But he giveth more grace. Wherefore he saith, God resisteth the proud, but giveth grace unto the humble.

WORD STUDY

more—great

grace—favor; kindness; enablement; gift

therefore—for this reason; that is why; which is why (introduces the scriptural evidence for what the author has just said)

resisteth—to oppose; to set oneself against

proud—haughty; arrogant; proud in character

humble—lowly in spirit; humble in character

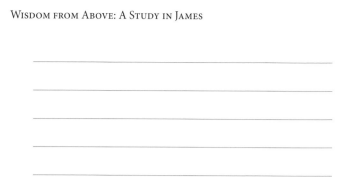

James introduces another thought concerning God's response to worldliness. God is not only jealous but also gracious. At this point many of us are overwhelmed because we recognize the amount of worldliness that resides in our hearts and comes out in our choices. However, instead of confirming us in despair, James gives us hope from God: "But He giveth more grace" (4:6). Douglas Moo says it well: "God's grace is completely adequate to meet the requirements imposed on us by that jealousy."[1]

God's grace is the supernatural enablement to do that which we cannot do ourselves.

There is no ambiguity in James's thoughts. He quotes Proverbs 3:34 to show us exactly how God responds to our choices: He resists the proud and gives grace to the humble. But what is grace? It is God's superabundant strength to live a life that overcomes the incredibly strong desires of one's evil nature. Living a committed Christian life in contrast to the world is beyond the strength of any Christian. God's grace is the supernatural enablement to do that which we cannot do ourselves. Grace says, "You can't, but God can."

Why do you think James cites Proverbs 3:34? What can you learn from the way James argues from Scripture?

Grace is unmerited favor. But just because God has an infinite supply of grace that He desires to give does not mean everyone gets it. None of us can earn it, but we must be humble to receive

[1] Douglas J. Moo, *The Letter of James*, The Pillar New Testament Commentary (Grand Rapids: Wm. Eerdmans Publishing Co., 2000), 191.

it. The word *resisteth* is like an army arranging itself in battle formation against an enemy. It isn't simply that God withholds grace from arrogant people. He actively opposes them. Relying on wisdom from below, fighting with other believers, being consumed with lust, adopting a worldly mindset—all of these sins greatly displease God. But the worst position any of us can be in is to be so infatuated with the world that we refuse to humble ourselves before our jealous, gracious God. Only those who wave the white flag, who prostrate themselves in utter dependence before the Lord, receive grace. And James drives home the importance of this humility by repeatedly emphasizing it in the next few verses.

In James 4:5–6 we see the two qualities of God at work in the restoration of the believer from the world. His jealousy convicts us of how we have strayed, and His grace enables us to return to Him in humble submission. God is truly more than enough!

In what ways do believers demonstrate pride? How does God resist us? Is He right and loving to do so?

In what ways are you tempted to have friendship with the world? How do the truths of God's jealousy and grace affect your outlook about this worldliness? What can you do to change?

Recommended Reading

Before beginning the next chapter, read Luke 18:9–17. In this passage the difference between pride and humility is eternally crucial. Describe how the men in this passage demonstrate either pride or humility.

8
GRACE THROUGH HUMILITY

JAMES 4:7–10

Submit yourselves therefore to God. Resist the devil, and he will flee from you. Draw nigh to God, and he will draw nigh to you. Cleanse your hands, ye sinners; and purify your hearts, ye double minded. Be afflicted, and mourn, and weep: let your laughter be turned to mourning, and your joy to heaviness. Humble yourselves in the sight of the Lord, and he shall lift you up.

Arthur Bennett has edited a wonderful collection of Puritan prayers entitled *The Valley of Vision*. In the introductory prayer by that same title, he writes:

> Let me learn by paradox
> that the way down is the way up,
> that to be low is to be high,
> that the broken heart is the healed heart,
> that the contrite spirit is the rejoicing spirit,
> that the repenting soul is the victorious soul,
> that to have nothing is to possess all,
> that to bear the cross is to wear the crown,
> that to give is to receive,
> that the valley is the place of vision.[1]

[1] Arthur Bennett, ed., *The Valley of Vision: A Collection of Puritan Prayers & Devotions* (Edinburgh: The Banner of Truth Trust, 1975), xxiv–xxv. (banneroftruth.org) Used by permission.

This prayer captures the essence of James's instruction for how to receive grace from God. Wisdom from above teaches us that God shows favor not to those who build themselves up but to those who make themselves low.

Every demand that God makes is met with His all-sufficient grace.

Every demand that God makes is met with His all-sufficient grace. He has more than enough grace to enable you to live a committed life. How do you receive it? By humility alone! Flowing directly from James's quotation of Proverbs 3:34, "God resisteth the proud, but giveth grace unto the humble" (4:6), is a series of ten commands. These imperatives center on the genuine humility through which God promises to give grace. These are an urgent call for his readers to take decisive action. If we have wavered between being friends of the world and the friends of God, we must make up our minds once and for all as to where our allegiance lies. Now is the time to get God's grace through humility.

We could study this passage in various ways. The first would be to consider these commands as ten separate imperatives. Our understanding, however, would be somewhat limited because these commands are interconnected. They comprise a series of steps in humbling oneself before God. The second approach would be to survey these commands from the priest-prophet perspective. Since James is writing to a Hebrew audience, they would note within the first five commands the image of a priest coming to minister in the temple—"draw nigh to God," "cleanse your hands," and "purify your hearts" (4:8). Within the last five commands, we see the depiction of an Old Testament prophet crying out against the sins of God's people and calling them to repentance—"be afflicted," "mourn," and "weep" (4:9). The third approach would be to view the first and last commands—"submit yourselves therefore to God" and "humble yourselves in the sight of the Lord"—as bookends. These two imperatives introduce and summarize the overall truth that grace is received through humility. The rest of the commands divide into three couplets that further explain the theme. We will follow this last approach by studying the overarching imperatives in this chapter and then the explanatory ones in the following chapter.

Although our study will not focus on the perspectives of priest and prophet, how could understanding the functions of a priest and a prophet contribute to our understanding of how God gives grace to His people?

The church father Augustine once prayed, "Give what you command, and then command whatever you will."[2] How does this petition capture the relationship between God's will and God's enablement? How can you apply this paradox personally?

[2] Augustine, *Confessions*, trans. F. J. Sheed (Indianapolis: Hackett Publishing Company, 1993, repr., 2006), 187.

The First Command

JAMES 4:7
Submit yourselves therefore to God.

WORD STUDY

submit—to be subjected; to enlist under; to surrender one's will, leading to obedience

The first command, "submit yourselves therefore to God" (4:7) introduces; the last command, "humble yourselves" (4:10), summarizes the primary actions God requires to receive His grace. *Submission* describes a soldier who enlists in the military, swears allegiance to his country, and puts himself in subordination (literally, "to rank under") to the authority of his commanding officer. The soldier's will is in complete subjection to the captain's will.

A survey of how the New Testament writers use the word *submit* provides additional context for understanding its meaning. First, various references emphasize that God is in complete control. Nothing escapes the reach of His sovereignty. The seventy disciples whom Jesus sent out to minister in His name returned with excitement because they commanded the submission of even demons in Christ's power (Luke 10:17). In Paul's exposition of the resurrection in 1 Corinthians 15 he declares that God the Father is subjecting all creation to the rule of His Son. This reality has sweeping, universal significance. It also has very personal implications. You lie at the heart of God's master plan to bring everything under the gracious rule of Jesus Christ.

In order to meditate on the truth that God is placing the entire universe under the feet of His Son, read Psalm 110:1 and Matthew 28:18–20. Why are these passages significant?

Second, we are not by nature submissive. In Romans 8:7 we are told that our flesh is at war with God and will not submit to Him. Therefore, we need God's grace to surrender ourselves to God's rule. God provides a metaphor for submission in the ancient practice of bond-slavery. Several passages refer to the necessity of slaves submitting themselves to their masters (Titus 2:9; 1 Pet. 2:18). The New Testament does not commend slavery, especially slavery of the sort that casts such a dark shadow over American history. However, God does command His people to honor those in authority over us. And the picture of a bondslave submitting to his master helps us understand how unreservedly we must serve the Lord. Just as Roman landlords had complete command over the lives of their slaves, so too God must have complete control over our lives. And the amazing truth is that this submission is not only the right approach to life—it is the only one that truly brings joy.

Are there areas of your life that you are not submitting to God? If so, why? How can you get grace from God to honor Him in these areas?

Third, several passages teach that our relationships with others relate to our submission to God. The first occurrence of this word *submit* refers to Jesus' submission to imperfect human parents, even though as Son of God, He was also their Creator (Luke 2:51). This isn't the last time Scripture speaks about submission within a home. God uses family relationships as both a testing ground and an illustration of our need to submit to His loving rule. It is a testing ground because through appropriate submission in contexts like the home we demonstrate that God's Spirit fills, or controls, us (Eph. 5:18). However, Paul's teaching on submission in the home is not simply a premarital counseling text. He describes how a wife's submission to the loving leadership of her husband is a picture of the church's submission to the perfect, sanctifying rule of Christ (5:24). By submitting to God, we are not subjecting ourselves to an ogre or a totalitarian but rather to a perfect ruler. And He is a loving father too. If we appropriately give respect to a well-meaning earthly father who helps us live successfully by disciplining us, how much more should we submit ourselves to "the Father of spirits" (Heb. 12:9)? His plans are far greater and His love far deeper.

Discuss the relationship between submitting to authorities God has placed over you and submitting to God Himself.

The Last Command

JAMES 4:10
Humble yourselves in the sight of the Lord, and he shall lift you up.

WORD STUDY

humble—make yourself low

before—in the presence of; in the sight of; in front of

exalt—to lift or raise up

Humility is depicted in one lying prostrate at the feet of a sovereign king. The subject senses his own unworthiness in the presence of the majesty of his ruler and waits dependently on his king to raise him up. A humble believer acknowledges God's authority and his need of God's favor. A grace-filled life overcomes worldliness not through self-effort but by full and complete surrender to God. Failure is unavoidable and defeat is inevitable if we operate according to our own natural abilities, limited resources, and human wisdom. Instead, we must cast ourselves in total dependence on God. Success is not a matter of performance but of reverence.

Part of what it means to follow Christ is to adopt His humility.

We noted in the introductory chapter that James's letter bears many resemblances to the teaching of his half-brother, Jesus. In one of His most memorable calls to discipleship, Christ stated, "Come unto me, all ye that labour and are heavy laden, and I will give you rest. Take my yoke upon you, and learn of me; for I am meek and lowly in heart: and ye shall find rest unto your souls" (Matt. 11:28–29). The word translated *lowly* is the adjective form of the verb that is translated *humble yourselves* in James 4:10. In other words, part of what it means to follow Christ is to adopt His humility. Rest for our souls is not found in achievement but in dependence on Him who bore our burdens all the way to the cross. As Bennett acknowledges in his prayer, "The broken heart is the healed heart."[3] Spiritual strength and vitality flow through the gates of submission and humility.

How are the commands to submit to God and to be humble before God similar? How are they different?

Read 2 Corinthians 12:7–10. What do humility and submission have to do with trials and weakness? In what present circumstances can you apply these truths?

[3] Bennett, xv.

Recommended Reading

Before beginning the next chapter, read 1 Peter 5:1–11. Show how Peter's instruction parallels James 4. Also, note the relationship between verses 6 and 7 in 1 Peter 5.

9
HUMILITY IN ACTION

JAMES 4:7–10

Submit yourselves therefore to God. Resist the devil, and he will flee from you. Draw nigh to God, and he will draw nigh to you. Cleanse your hands, ye sinners; and purify your hearts, ye double minded. Be afflicted, and mourn, and weep: let your laughter be turned to mourning, and your joy to heaviness. Humble yourselves in the sight of the Lord, and he shall lift you up.

Pride shows up in the chest-beating celebration of a professional athlete and the swagger of a savvy lawyer. It looks like the air of superiority some exude toward those of other ethnicities or the dismissive sneer of a smug scholar. It is fairly easy to spot pride in other people but rather difficult to recognize and reject it personally. But if pride precipitates destruction (Prov. 16:18), we must soberly assess our propensity for it and actively pursue a life of humility. Drawing from the teaching of John Owen, J. I. Packer writes, "Self-confidence and self-satisfaction argue self-ignorance. The only healthy Christian is the humble, broken-hearted Christian."[1]

In the previous chapter we discovered that God grants us grace as we submit ourselves to Him in humility. In this chapter we need to delve more deeply into what this humility looks like. Sometimes we view humility as being quiet or

[1] J. I. Packer, *A Quest for Godliness: The Puritan Vision of the Christian Life* (Wheaton: Crossway Books, 1990), 196.

being critical of ourselves. But Scripture speaks of humility as a God-dependent mindset that displays itself through certain pursuits. With the commands in between "submit yourselves" (4:7) and "humble yourselves" (4:10), James paints a portrait of a humble response to God's rebuke about worldliness. Just as true faith is active (see James 2), true humility is also active. The humble Christian pursues divine fellowship, which requires spiritual cleansing and begins with godly sorrow.

Fellowship with God Instead of the Devil

JAMES 4:7–8

. . . Resist the devil, and he will flee from you.
Draw nigh to God, and he will draw nigh to you.

WORD STUDY

resist—to withstand or stand up against; to stand up to; to set oneself against

flee—to run away; to take flight

draw near—to approach; to come close; a return to communion with God

The first set of commands involves our position relative to God and to Satan. Negatively, we are to take a stance in opposition to the Devil—"Resist the devil" (4:7). Believers whom God formerly resisted because of their pride (4:6) are now commanded to resist the influences of the Devil. Remember, it is this Devil's world with which James' readers had become intimate friends (4:4). Opposing Satan involves positioning ourselves defensively against his attacks (Eph. 6:10–19). Christ demonstrated this in real life as He withstood the Devil's temptations in the wilderness (Matt. 4:1–11). James's readers would have to reject the earthly wisdom that produced envy and selfish ambition (James 3:14–16).

We must realize that our allegiance to God means, in part, that we will face the attacks of Satan. We are naturally fearful to stand up against someone who is armed to fight and defeat us, and Satan is a real adversary. He prowls around looking for opportunities to devour us (1 Pet. 5:8). He has schemes that he hurls like fiery darts against us (Eph. 6:11). Part of humbling ourselves is having a sober awareness of the real danger of a real Devil and committing ourselves to oppose him by standing strong in the strength of our Savior (1 Pet. 5:8; Eph. 6:10, 13).

Read Matthew 4:1–11. What devices or schemes did Satan use in tempting Jesus? How did Jesus respond?

Positively, we are to cultivate a close fellowship with God—“Draw nigh to God” (4:8). Like an Old Testament priest who drew close to the presence of God as he entered into the temple, so God commands believers to come close to Him. But how can we have true communion with an infinitely holy God? We can come directly into His glorious presence because of the sacrifice and cleansing blood of Christ (Heb. 10:19–22). We can boldly approach God’s throne of grace (Heb. 4:16), because Christ boldly entered the holy of holies with a perfect, one-time sacrifice to atone for our sin (Heb. 10:19).

Look at Hebrews 10:19–25. Notice the three exhortations that begin with the words “let us.”

What does the third exhortation have to do with the first two?

Spiritual warfare is just as real as your next meal, but it cannot be waged successfully with mere human strength.

Spiritual warfare is just as real as your next meal (Eph. 6:12), but it cannot be waged successfully with mere human strength. We need divine power (2 Cor. 10:4–5). That is why both opposing the Devil and living close to God are impossible without consistent Bible reading, prayer, worship, and intimate fellowship with other believers. We cannot view these habits as ways to gain God's favor but as channels through which He supplies grace. They are God's appointed weapons for victory. Notice that in both commands, there is a corresponding response to the believer's obedience. In the case of the Devil, he will take flight and run away from us. In the case of God, He will come close to us as we seek to come close to Him. God will fulfill His promise of giving us grace as we humble ourselves in relationship to Him and to the Devil.

What fiery darts (i.e., temptations) are you facing right now? How can you resist the Devil?

According to Ephesians 6:13–18, what weaponry has God provided for you to stand strong in faith?

Purity Outwardly and Inwardly

JAMES 4:8

. . . Cleanse your hands, ye sinners; and purify your hearts, ye double minded.

WORD STUDY

cleanse—to make clean; implies personal duty to confess and forsake sins

purify—to purge; to see that something is pure

heart—inner self

double-minded—doubting or wavering, having mixed motives; unstable or fickle

The second set of commands involves thorough, ongoing purification in our lives. Outwardly, we are commanded to clean up our actions: "Cleanse your hands, ye sinners." James is calling his readers *sinners*, not because they were unsaved, but because he wanted to expose the true nature of their desires and choices. Their actions were being driven by their passion to find satisfaction and fulfillment in the world, just like unbelieving sinners who live "according to the course of this world" (Eph. 2:2–3). Consequently, sin was very much alive in their lives. In order to remove the stains of the world, cleansing was absolutely necessary. When we live according to worldly wisdom and adopt worldly affinities, James calls us to confess our sins and turn from our worldly behavior. This summons resembles Isaiah's prophetic message to Israel seven centuries earlier:

> Wash you, make you clean; put away the evil of your doings from before mine eyes; cease to do evil. (Isa. 1:16)

It is frequently said that what matters is the heart, and for good reason. Jesus taught, "That which cometh out of the man, that defileth the man" (Mark 7:20). How does James's exhortation about our actions complement this truth?

Inwardly, we are commanded by James to purify our thoughts and motives: "Purify your hearts, ye double minded" (4:8). *Double-minded* (literally, *double-souled*) indicates a divided loyalty between God and the world. The only answer for this dual spiritual allegiance is genuine purging of self-centered motives.

These commands show that the process of purification is the responsibility of every Christian. James may have Psalm 24 in view, where David asks the question, "Who shall ascend into the hill of the Lord? or who shall stand in his holy place?" (24:3). The first part of his answer is "He that hath clean hands, and a pure heart" (24:4). Those who desire to dwell with God cannot take their sin lightly, whether thoughts or words or actions. God calls for wholehearted commitment and single-focused living for His glory. Is the kind of purity David describes possible? Can we cleanse our own hands or purify our own hearts? We cannot sanctify ourselves, but we can come to Christ for cleansing, and we must. Consider Hebrews 9:13–14.

> For if the blood of bulls and of goats, and the ashes of an heifer sprinkling the unclean, sanctifieth to the purifying of the flesh: how much more shall the blood of Christ, who through the eternal Spirit offered himself without spot to God, purge your conscience from dead works to serve the living God?

Jesus taught that no one "can serve two masters" (Matt. 6:24). James speaks to Christians who are double-minded. How do these two passages relate to one another? Why is this significant?

Repentance Instead of Carelessness

JAMES 4:9

Be afflicted, and mourn, and weep: let your laughter be turned to mourning, and your joy to heaviness.

WORD STUDY

be afflicted—to be sorrowful; to be miserable; to make oneself wretched and weep in misery over sin

mourn—to be sad; to grieve; to weep; refers to the outward demeanor of those who grieve inwardly

weep—to sob; to cry; to sorrow tearfully over sin

mourning—sorrow; sadness; grief

turned—changed inwardly by another's power

heaviness—dejection; gloominess; despair

The last set of commands is a serious call to deep, heartfelt repentance. We must respond to our sin with a spirit of genuine remorse. Paul calls it "godly sorrow" in 2 Corinthians 7:10. James announces like an Old Testament prophet the appropriate heart attitudes that accompany repentance. The first three commands denote the depths of sorrow believers should manifest. To *be afflicted* is to suffer a wretched feeling of misery. James calls for a deep, inner sense of distress and shame over sin. To *mourn* is to display the intense grief and sadness one feels concerning his sin, a grief often displayed at a funeral. To *weep* includes the crying and sobbing of one whose heart has been broken over sin. Again, these commands echo an earlier Scripture:

> Therefore also now, saith the Lord, turn ye even to me with all your heart, and with fasting, and with weeping, and with mourning. (Joel 2:12)

Use James's admonitions along with what Paul says in 2 Corinthians 7 to list some distinctions between godly sorrow and mere earthly sorrow.

Christ said that this mourning is a proper spiritual attitude (Matt. 5:4). Peter manifested all of these attitudes when he denied the Lord and afterward went out and wept bitterly over his sin (Luke 22:62). The last command calls for a noticeable change in public expressions. “Let your laughter be turned to mourning, and your joy to heaviness” (4:9). When we are close to God, we feel gravity about sin; but when we are worldly, our attitude is more carefree and nonchalant—an attitude that needs to change! The imperative *turn* means to turn around or reverse direction. *Laughter* is the outward expression of a lighthearted attitude toward sins. Spiritually shallow believers seek joy in the world’s desires; but in contrast, genuine change comes only through mourning over sin. The tax collector exemplified this response when he entered the temple to pray and would not even lift up his eyes to God because of his shame. In a public yet humble response, he beat upon his chest over his sin (Luke 18:13).

So what happens when these commands are obeyed? The result is a deep sense of humility before God and a heart genuinely broken over sin. When we are in this position, God responds in grace by lifting us up and restoring us to a place of friendship with God. We must draw near to Him while resisting the Devil. We must seek both inward and outward purity. We must truly repent of our sins. Godly sorrow is a litmus test of humility.

When we are close to God, we feel gravity about sin.

Are there behaviors or words or thoughts for which you need cleansing? If so, don't finish this chapter without running to Christ.

Discuss the progression of submission and humility to godly repentance. Why is godly sorrow over sin essential to overcoming worldliness? When is the last time you experienced godly sorrow over your sin?

Recommended Reading

Before beginning the next chapter, read James 3:13–4:10 to review what this passage teaches. List what you have learned.

10
THE PATH OF WISDOM FROM ABOVE

PSALMS 1:1–2

Blessed is the man that walketh not in the counsel of the ungodly, nor standeth in the way of sinners, nor sitteth in the seat of the scornful. But his delight is in the law of the Lord; and in his law doth he meditate day and night.

Psalms—the world's most important book of poetry—begins with a picturesque contrast of two paths: the way of the righteous and the way of the wicked. According to Psalm 1, a blessed person distinguishes himself by delighting in God's Word instead of listening to worldly counsel (1:1–2). Rather than curiously mulling over ungodly advice, he meditates on revealed truth "day and night." The Hebrew word translated *meditate* conveys intense consideration, to the point of muttering or repeating words over and over.

Bible meditation in our fast-paced, technology-fueled society is not easy. It's an uphill climb with plenty of challenging crosswinds. We process so many texts and tweets and ten-second video clips that we have hardly any time or attention left. But the strength that develops in a heart full of God's loving truth surpasses any ease offered by any other route. That's why our study in James includes this final chapter. We need to retrace our steps and recall the features of this path of wisdom from above. Reviewing the message and themes of this passage will renew our minds so that we can be "doers of the word, and not hearers only" (James 1:22).

Recognizing Divine Wisdom

JAMES 3:13–18

> Who is a wise man and endued with knowledge among you? let him shew out of a good conversation his works with meekness of wisdom. But if ye have bitter envying and strife in your hearts, glory not, and lie not against the truth. This wisdom descendeth not from above, but is earthly, sensual, devilish. For where envying and strife is, there is confusion and every evil work. But the wisdom that is from above is first pure, then peaceable, gentle, and easy to be intreated, full of mercy and good fruits, without partiality, and without hypocrisy. And the fruit of righteousness is sown in peace of them that make peace.

Interstate highways are a marvelous invention. They facilitate efficient, direct travel between major cities, as long as you are heading in the right direction. Have you ever experienced that sickening realization that you've been driving the wrong way for a while? Perhaps you noticed landmarks you had never seen before. Maybe the digitized GPS voice cleverly uttered that dreaded word, "Recalculating."

James writes as one of the early church leaders in Jerusalem to Jewish Christians so that they might become spiritually mature. And this maturity necessitates wisdom from above. In the final paragraph of James 3, he raises the question of how to identify a wise person and then describes the telltale signs. If we slow down and notice our surroundings, we will understand whether or not we are obtaining and employing God's wisdom. Or to change the analogy, there is unmistakable fruit. We recognize the source of wisdom by the fruit it bears in everyday life.

We must assess the fruit that is coming from our lives personally and collectively. On one hand, wisdom from below produces jealousy and sinful ambition, which lead to chaos and many manifestations of evil. On the other hand, wisdom from above demonstrates itself in both actions and attitudes. It leads to purity and peace, to reasonableness and gentleness and compassion, to consistency and sincerity. God structured life to work when we prayerfully and humbly apply His knowledge to our everyday circumstances.

God structured life to work when we prayerfully and humbly apply His knowledge to our everyday circumstances.

How are your relationships going? What kind of wisdom do they display?

Acknowledging Worldly Affections

JAMES 4:1–5

From whence come wars and fightings among you? come they not hence, even of your lusts that war in your members? Ye lust, and have not: ye

> kill, and desire to have, and cannot obtain: ye fight and war, yet ye have not, because ye ask not. Ye ask, and receive not, because ye ask amiss, that ye may consume it upon your lusts. Ye adulterers and adulteresses, know ye not that the friendship of the world is enmity with God? whosoever therefore will be a friend of the world is the enemy of God. Do ye think that the scripture saith in vain, The spirit that dwelleth in us lusteth to envy?

At the beginning of James 4, the author exposes the reasons his readers were acting selfishly and sensually. Professing Christians may fight for petty reasons, such as the auditorium carpet color or preferred slots on the offertory schedule. But even the most ridiculous squabbling has underlying causes. James calls them *lusts*. These lusts are the fleshly desires we seek to fulfill in unlawful, unloving ways. When we ignore God's wisdom, we give way to powerful cravings corrupted by sin. And when we interact with one another, our uncontrolled desires produce conflicts and fighting.

God has given us resources to access His wisdom, but like James's readers, we often fail to make use of them. We do not experience victory over sinful passions because we do not pray. And when we do pray, many times our motives distort our petitions. We pray for what we want with little thought of what God wants. "Envying and strife . . . confusion and every evil work" (3:16) are not the results of incompatible personalities or age differences or budget deficiencies. God's people fight because our flesh puts itself above God's kingdom and people.

It is one thing to admit we fight because we are selfish. It is another to acknowledge that our affection for this world makes us enemies of God. James minces no words. Although he refers to his readers as *brothers* fifteen times in his letter, in this paragraph James calls them *adulterers* and *adulteresses* (4:4).

The sinful desires that go unchecked and burst into skirmishes with others expose disloyalty to our Savior. We cannot serve God and the world simultaneously. As the hymn writer testified, "Prone to wander, Lord, I feel it, prone to leave the God I love."[1] This spiritual adultery is serious, just like it was for Israel to worship Canaanite gods. It arouses the jealousy of the spirit God put within us. We belong to Him. But when we do not seek wisdom from above, trailing off the path and flirting with the spirit of our age seem okay.

Discuss some examples of how our fleshly desires contribute to conflict with other believers. Discuss if and how prayer could make a difference.

Submitting to Transforming Grace

JAMES 4:6–10

But he giveth more grace. Wherefore he saith, God resisteth the proud, but giveth grace unto the humble. Submit yourselves therefore to God. Resist the devil, and he will flee from you. Draw nigh to God, and he will draw nigh to you. Cleanse your hands, ye sinners; and purify your hearts, ye double minded. Be afflicted, and mourn, and weep: let your laughter be turned to mourning,

[1] Robert Robinson, "Come, Thou Fount of Every Blessing" (1757).

> and your joy to heaviness. Humble yourselves in the sight of the Lord, and he shall lift you up.

Even though his indictment of spiritual adultery is scathing, James does not leave us without hope. Paired with the righteous jealousy of God is His abundant grace. God knows that we are sinful people laden with fleshly desires that will not be remedied this side of glory. As a lovingly jealous husband, He is neither indifferent to our sin nor willing to let us go and perish. He gives us grace as we humble ourselves. He is high and holy, but He chooses to dwell with the contrite and lowly (Isa. 57:15).

Those who are humble before the Lord strongly oppose the Devil.

But how do we know if we are humble? What does it look like to submit ourselves to God and renew our minds in His wisdom? James sketches an active portrait of humility. Those who are humble before the Lord strongly oppose the Devil (just as God strongly opposes the proud). At the same time, the humble seek close fellowship with the God to whom they have been disloyal. We experience this renewed relationship through purity, both in our hearts and in our lifestyle, and repentance. Pride seeks to avoid consequences. Humility seeks restoration whatever the cost. God has more than enough transforming grace for those who humbly submit to Him.

Sometimes we view humility as the absence of outrageous vanity and boasting. But evaluating our pride should go much deeper than such surface observations. Consider the following questions:

Am I a critical and gossiping person?

Do I regularly question authority?

Do I make fun of weaker, less-privileged people?

Do I treat people differently based on their status?

Am I dissatisfied with God's Word as sufficient for life and godliness?

Do I make plans without making the Lord the center of my focus?

Do I shift blame instead of taking responsibility for my actions?

Do I widely proclaim my views but rarely listen?

Do I hold grudges instead of extending forgiveness?

Do I put up a front instead of confessing my faults to those who can help?

Do I pray sparingly?

The point of these questions[2] is not to drive you simply to do better. Answering yes to some of these questions is the first step toward repentance and receiving God's grace, because a humble person is honest. He understands what David confessed—that God wants us to have integrity in our hearts (Ps. 51:6). Recognizing spiritual unfaithfulness and pride does not mean we pull ourselves up by our own bootstraps. It means running to Christ for superabundant grace. It means humbling ourselves to get back on the path of wisdom from above.

[2] Questions adapted from a Sunday school lesson by Jim Wiginton, Mt. Calvary Baptist Church, Greenville, SC, May 3, 2015.